THE BABY ANIMAL BOOK

JENNIFER COSSINS

LOTHIAN
Children's Books

A Lothian Children's Book

This edition published in Australia and New Zealand in 2017
by Hachette Australia
Level 17, 207 Kent Street, Sydney NSW 2000
www.hachettechildrens.com.au

First published in Australia and New Zealand in 2015
by Red Parka Press

1 3 5 7 9 10 8 6 4 2

National Library of Australia Cataloguing-in-Publication data

Cossins, Jennifer, author.
The baby animal book / Jennifer Cossins

ISBN 978 0 7344 1815 9 (HB)
ISBN 978 0 7344 1816 6 (PB)

Animals–Infancy–Juvenile literature.
Animals–Pictorial works–Juvenile literature.
Picture books for children.

Designed by Red Parka Press
Printed in China by Toppan Leefung Printing Limited

THIS BOOK IS FOR
JO-MAREE, CHARLES,
FRASER, CAMERON & MAGGIE COURTNEY.

ALSO MY SWEET BOYS OBERON AND BENNY,
FOREVER LOVED AND NEVER FORGOTTEN.

A BABY CAT IS CALLED A KITTEN

A BABY GOOSE
IS CALLED
A GOSLING

A BABY DEER IS CALLED A FAWN

A BABY OWL IS CALLED AN OWLET

A BABY ELEPHANT IS CALLED A CALF

A BABY FOX IS CALLED A KIT

A BABY POLAR BEAR IS CALLED A CUB

A BABY DOG
IS CALLED
A PUPPY

A BABY TASMANIAN DEVIL IS CALLED AN IMP

A BABY ORANGUTAN IS CALLED AN INFANT

A BABY HAWK
IS CALLED
AN EYAS

A BABY KANGAROO IS CALLED A JOEY

A BABY PEACOCK
IS CALLED
A PEACHICK

A BABY PRAYING MANTIS IS CALLED A NYMPH

A BABY PENGUIN IS CALLED A CHICK

A BABY
PARTRIDGE
IS CALLED
A CHEEPER

A BABY PLATYPUS IS CALLED A PUGGLE

A BABY PUFFIN IS CALLED A PUFFLING

A BABY SEAL
IS CALLED
A PUP

A BABY SWAN
IS CALLED
A CYGNET

A BABY WOLF
IS CALLED
A WHELP

ALSO BY JENNIFER COSSINS

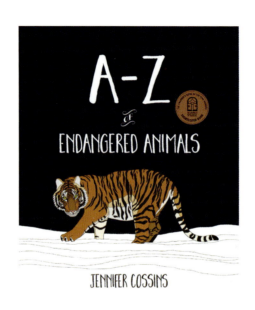

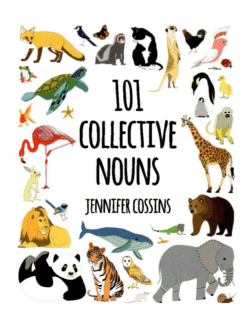

ABOUT THE AUTHOR

Jennifer Cossins is a Tasmanian artist and writer with a passion for nature, the animal kingdom and all things bright and colourful.

A born and bred Tasmanian, Jennifer also designs homewares, textiles and stationery, which she stocks in her store, Red Parka, in Hobart, Tasmania.

Jennifer's other books include *A–Z of Endangered Animals* and *101 Collective Nouns*.

REDPARKA.COM.AU

THE END